Melody Beattie

GRATITUDE

Affirming the Good Things in Life

Inspiring Passages from her
best-sellers *Codependent No More,*
Beyond Codependency, and
The Language of Letting Go

HAZELDEN

Published by MJF Books
Fine Communications
Two Lincoln Square
60 West 66th Street
New York, NY 10023

Gratitude
ISBN 1-56731-367-1

Printed by arrangement with Hazelden Foundation.

Editor's Note: Hazelden Educational Materials offers a variety of
information on chemical dependency and related areas. Our
publications do not necessarily represent Hazelden's programs, nor
do they officially speak for any Twelve Step organizations.

10   9   8   7   6   5   4   3   2   1

GRATITUDE:
Affirming the Good
Things in Life

INTRODUCTION

Sometimes in life things happen too fast. We barely solve one problem when two new problems surface. We're feeling great in the morning, but we're submerged in misery by nightfall.

Every day we face interruptions, delays, changes, and challenges. We face personality conflicts and disappointments. Often when we're feeling overwhelmed, we can't see the lessons in these experiences.

One simple concept can get us through the most stressful of times. It's called *gratitude*. We learn to say *thank you* for these problems and feelings. *Thank you* for the way things are. I don't like this experience, but *thank you* anyway.

Gratitude unlocks the fullness of life. Gratitude makes things right. It turns what we have into enough, and more. It turns denial into acceptance, chaos to order, confusion to clarity. It can turn a meal into a feast, a house into a home, a stranger into a friend. It turns problems into gifts, failures into successes, the unexpected into perfect timing, and mistakes into important events. It can turn an existence into a real life, and disconnected situations into important and beneficial lessons. Gratitude makes sense of our past, brings peace for today, and creates a vision for tomorrow.

In the following pages you'll see how deprived thinking turns good things into less or nothing, and how grateful thinking turns all things into more. You'll see how you can use affirmations to move from feeling deprived to deserving. And, finally, we'll talk about enhancing the good things in your life by tapping in to these basic human skills: self-care, acceptance, setting goals, communication, and making decisions.

Gratitude turns negative energy into positive energy. We can start with who we are and what we have *today*, apply gratitude, then let it work its magic. There is no situation or circumstance so small or large that it is not susceptible to gratitude's power. This is a book to remind you of that power.

Affirming the Gratitude Principle

$\mathcal{M}$any of us were deprived as children, but many of us have also carried that deprivation into adulthood. Deprivation creates deprived thinking. Deprived thinking perpetuates deprivation.

Many of us know how easy it is to fall into the trap of short-supply thinking. We think, *There's good stuff out there, but there isn't enough for me.* We may become desperate, scrambling to get what we can and holding tightly to it, whether or not it is what we want or is good for us. We may become resentful and jealous of people who have enough. We may hoard what we have or refuse to enjoy it, fearing we'll use it up. We may give up and settle for less. Deprivation becomes habitual. We may continue to feel afraid and deprived, even when we're not.

Examine Your Beliefs

We may react to deprivation in many ways. We may insist that life, and the people in our lives, make up for all we never had. That's unfair, and those expectations can wreck what's good today.

Deprived, negative thinking makes things disappear. We grumble about the half-empty water glass, so focused on what we don't have that we fail to appreciate all that we do have—the half-full glass of water, the glass itself, or being alive and well enough to drink the water. We become so afraid that we might not get more, or we're so sour about having only half a glass to drink, that we may not even drink it. We let it sit on the table until it evaporates. Then we have nothing, which is what we thought we had anyway. It's an illusion! We can drink the water if we're thirsty, then go to the tap and get more.

Perhaps the most profound effect of deprivation is that we may decide we don't deserve the good things in life. This isn't true, but our belief will make it seem true. What we believe we deserve—what we really believe deep inside—will be what we get.

Deprived, negative thinking can prevent us from seeing what's good in our lives today, and it can stop the good stuff from happening. It hurts to be deprived. It hurts to walk through life believing there's not enough. It's painful to believe we're undeserving. So, stop. Now. Tell yourself, "There's enough." There is enough for you. There's even enough for the person next door, too. Tell yourself, "I deserve." You deserve the best, whatever that means for you. And you can start affirming this today.

Turn What You Have Into More

Deprived thinking turns good things into less, or worse, into nothing. Grateful thinking turns things into more.

Many years ago, I dreamed of getting married and raising a family. I also dreamed of owning a house, a beautiful home that would be our little castle. I wanted some of the things other people had. I wanted "normal," whatever that was.

It looked like I was about to get it, too. I got married. I got pregnant. I had a baby girl. Now, all I needed was the home. We looked at all sorts of dream homes—big dream homes and in-between dream homes. The home we bought didn't turn out to be one of those, but it was the one we could afford.

It had been used as rental property for fifteen years and had been standing vacant for a year. Now it was three stories of broken windows and broken wood. Some rooms had ten layers of wallpaper on the walls. Some walls had holes straight through to the outdoors. The floors were covered with bright orange carpeting with large stains. And we didn't have money or skills to fix it. We had no money for windows, curtains, paint. We couldn't afford to furnish it. We had three stories of a dilapidated home, with a kitchen table, two chairs, a high chair, a bed, a crib, and two dressers, one of which had broken drawers.

About two weeks after we moved in, a friend stopped by. We stood talking on what would have been the lawn if grass had been growing there. My friend kept repeating how lucky I was and how nice it was to own your own home. But I didn't feel lucky, and it didn't feel nice. I didn't know anyone else who owned a home like this.

I didn't talk much about how I felt, but each night while my husband and daughter slept, I tiptoed down to the living room, sat on the floor, and cried. This became a ritual. When everyone was asleep, I sat in the middle of the floor thinking about everything I hated about the house, crying, and feeling hopeless. I did this for months. However legitimate my reaction may have been, it changed nothing.

A few times, in desperation, I tried to fix up the house, but nothing worked. The day before Thanksgiving I attempted to paint the living and dining room walls. But layers of wallpaper started to peel off the minute I put paint on them. Another time, I ordered expensive wallpaper, trying to have faith that I'd have the money to pay for it when it came. I didn't.

Then one evening, when I was sitting in the middle of the floor going through my wailing ritual, a thought occurred to me: *Why don't I try gratitude?*

At first I dismissed the idea. Gratitude was absurd. What could I possibly be grateful for? How could I? And why should I? Then I decided to try anyway. I had nothing to lose. And I was getting sick of my whining.

Acknowledge What You Have

I still wasn't certain what to be grateful for, so I decided to be grateful for everything. I didn't *feel* grateful. I willed it. I forced it. I faked it. I pretended. I made myself think grateful thoughts. When I thought about the layers of peeling wallpaper, I thanked God. I thanked God for each thing I hated about that house. I thanked God for giving it to me. I thanked God that I was there. I even thanked God that I hated it. Each time I had a negative thought about the house, I countered it with a grateful one.

Maybe this wasn't as logical a reaction as being negative, but it turned out to be much more effective. After I practiced gratitude for about three or four months, things started to change.

My attitude changed. I stopped spending my nights sitting and crying in the middle of the floor and started to accept the house—as it was. I started taking care of the house as though it were a dream home. I acted as if it were my dream home. I kept it clean and orderly, as nice as could be.

Then I started thinking: If I took all the old wallpaper off first, maybe the paint would stay on. I pulled up some of the orange carpeting and discovered solid oak floors throughout the house. I went through some of the boxes I had packed away and found antique lace curtains that fit the windows. I found a community-action program that sold decent wallpaper for a dollar a roll. I learned about textured paint, the kind that fills and covers old, cracked walls. I decided if I didn't know how to do the work,

I could learn. My mother volunteered to help me with the wallpapering. Everything I needed began to come to me.

Nine months later, I had a beautiful home. Solid oak floors glistened throughout the house. Country-print wallpaper and textured white walls contrasted beautifully with the dark, scrolled woodwork that decorated each room.

Whenever I encountered a problem—half the cupboard doors were missing and I didn't have money to hire a carpenter—I willed gratitude. Pretty soon, a solution appeared: tear all the doors off and have an open, country kitchen pantry.

I worked and worked, and in time I had three floors of beautiful home. It wasn't perfect, but it was mine and I was happy to be there. Proud to be there. Truly grateful to be there. I loved that home.

Soon the house filled up with furniture, too. I learned to selectively collect pieces here and there for $5 and $10, to cover the flaws with lace doilies, and to refinish. I learned how to make something out of almost nothing, instead of nothing out of something.

Since then I have had the opportunity to practice

the gratitude principle many times in my life. It has never failed me. Either I change, my circumstances change, or both change.

You Deserve the Best

"But you don't know how deprived I am!" people say. "You don't know everything I've gone without. You don't know how difficult it is right now. You don't know what it's like to have nothing!"

Yes, I do. And gratitude is the solution. Being grateful for what we have today doesn't mean we have to have that forever. It means we acknowledge that what we have today is what we're supposed to have today. There is enough. We're enough. And all we need will come to us. We don't have to be desperate, fearful, jealous, resentful, or miserly. We don't have to worry about what someone else has; they don't have what is ours. All we need to do is appreciate and take care of what we have today. The trick is, we need to be grateful first—before we get anything else, not afterward.

We need to believe that we deserve the best life has to offer. If we don't believe that, we need to change what we believe we deserve. Changing our beliefs about what we deserve isn't an overnight process. Whether we're talking about relationships, work, home, or money, this usually happens in increments. We believe we deserve something a little better, then a little better than that, and so on. We need to start right where we're at, changing our beliefs as we're able. Sometimes things take time.

Believing we deserve good things is as important as gratitude. Practicing gratitude without changing what we believe we deserve may keep us stuck in deprivation.

"I earned $30,000 a year and every morning I got into my ten-year-old car with a busted heater and thanked God for it. I was so grateful," says one woman. "My kids would encourage me to buy a new car and I'd say no; I was just grateful to have my old one. Then one day, when I was talking to someone about deprivation, it hit me that I could afford to have a new car if I really believed I deserved one. I changed my mind about what I deserved, then went out and bought a new car."

There are times in our lives when depriving ourselves helps build character, renders us fit for certain purposes, or is part of "paying our dues" as we stretch toward achieving goals. But this sort of deprivation not only has a purpose, it also has a beginning and an end. Many of us carry this too far. Our deprivation is without purpose or end.

AFFIRM YOURSELF

I used to think affirmations were, well, silly. I have since changed my mind—and my life. I changed my mind because affirmations are a tool that helped me change my life.

To "affirm" means to say positively, declare firmly, or assert to be true. The concept of using affirmations is closely connected to another term, *empowerment*. To "empower" means to give ability to, enable, or permit.

Through the messages we received in our family of origin, through living with the "rules," being shamed, being deprived, many of us have developed a repertoire of negative ideas about ourselves, other people, and even about life. We may have said, thought, and believed these messages for years. We may have a disciplined ritual for chanting these messages. Many of us have repeated these beliefs so long that we've internalized them. The negative messages have become so embedded in our sub-conscious they have manifested themselves in our lives. They've become our premises, our truths, and therefore our reality.

We can, however, learn to develop a repertoire of positive ideas about ourselves, other people, and life. We can develop a disciplined ritual for chanting these new messages. We can begin to repeat these beliefs so often that we internalize them. And as these positive messages become embedded in our subconscious, they will begin to manifest themselves in our lives. They now become our premises, our truths, and therefore our reality. That's what affirmations help us do. They keep charging our battery as we change the energy in ourselves and our lives from negative to positive.

Affirmations are how we change the rules, change the messages, deal with shame. Affirmations are how we travel the road from deprived to deserving. We assert new beliefs to be true, give ourselves new permissions, make new messages, and endow ourselves with new abilities. We empower the good and the positive in ourselves and life. Affirmations aren't optional. They are the core of healthy living. If negative messages have contributed to this havoc, imagine what positive messages can help create!

Affirmations aren't silly little sayings or wishful thinking. They're the antidote to all the negative garbage we've been feeding ourselves for years.

Affirmations open the door to good things coming our way, and to the good already there.

Affirmations Help Create Reality

Using affirmations means replacing negative messages with positive ones: We change what we say so we can change what we see. If we emphasize and empower the good in ourselves, we will see and get more of that. If we empower the good in others, we will get more of that, too.

The power and responsibility to change our messages and beliefs—to affirm and empower ourselves—lies with each of us. During certain times in our lives we may need to rely on others to empower and affirm us. At low points in my life, certain people affirmed and empowered me, and it was a gift from God. I try to pass this gift on. I still need people to believe in me and empower me. It's good to do this for each other. And yet, it's when we begin affirming and empowering ourselves, that we make giant strides forward.

To empower means to give power to. What have we been giving power to? The terrible way we look? How bad we feel? Our problems? Another person's problem? Our lack of money, time, or talent? The awfulness of life? Next question: Do we really want to feed and nurture negative ideas—knowing those attitudes will likely create more negative ideas and negative reality? Do we want to empower the problem or the solution?

If our relationships have worked out badly, we may believe that relationships don't work, that there aren't any healthy people out there, and people always use us. We may joke about it. We may say it seriously. Or we may keep this thought to ourselves. But it becomes what we believe and expect. If we want to change what happens, we change what we believe and expect. We surrender to what was and is. We accept our present circumstances. However, we also create space for something different to happen in our lives.

A positive new affirmation might be: *There are good people out there. I am attracted to healthy, loving people, and they are attracted to me. A healthy relationship is on its way.* We don't obsess about this thought. We don't watch for it to happen. But we may want to think this new thought five times a day or whenever an old, negative thought occurs to us. Then we let go of the results. It doesn't matter whether anything happens today, tomorrow, or next week, we decide this will be our belief. And if something contrary to our new belief happens, we don't use the incident to prove our old belief was really true.

We change our family of origin rules and messages from negative to positive. For instance, we change *I'm not lovable* and *I can't take care of myself* to *I'm lovable* and *I can take care of myself.* We overpower the negative with an equally powerful positive message.

If shame is an issue for us, we might want to focus on the message *It's okay to be who I am. Who I am is good, and I'm good enough.* We change what we believe we deserve, too. What we want to affirm is dealer's choice. If we have believed that there are not enough good jobs, good men or women, money, or love to go around, we start claiming prosperity in those areas.

Our goal in using affirmations isn't to eliminate every negative thought and sad feeling from our lives. That is neither healthy nor desirable. We don't want to turn into robots. Feeling sad and angry is sometimes as important as feeling happy and peaceful.

What Affirmations Are and Are Not

Using affirmations doesn't mean we ignore problems. That's denial. We need to identify problems, but we need to empower solutions. Affirmations won't eliminate problems from our lives; affirmations will help solve them.

Affirmations aren't a substitute for accepting reality. They aren't a form of control. They need to be used with heavy doses of surrender, spirituality, and letting go.

Often, it feels awkward and uncomfortable when we start the process of changing negative messages to positive ones. Things may temporarily get worse. A room always looks dirtier when we start to clean it. We pull the unwanted items and trash out of the nooks and crannies. Cleaning intensifies the disorder, until a new order can be created.

It's normal to resist affirmations and positive thoughts. If you've been feeding yourself negative ideas for ten, twenty, or thirty years, of course the positive will feel strange for a while. Give yourself five or ten years of diligently and assertively affirming the good. It won't take that long to manifest itself in your life, but give it time anyway. Be patient. Don't give up. Don't let whatever problems or issues that arise reinforce your old, negative thought patterns.

You'll probably be tested when you turn negative beliefs into positive ones. Often, when I change a belief, a big tidal wave sweeps into my life to try to wash away my new belief. It's as if life is saying, "There! Now what do you *really* believe?" Let the storm roar. Hold fast to your new affirmations. Let them be your anchor. When the storm passes, you'll see you're on solid ground with new beliefs.

Nurturing
Ourselves

*S*ometimes the pressures and disappointments of daily life keep us from appreciating the small things in life, let alone the big gifts in life. These gifts include our health, our minds, our spirits—in other words, our very lives. Yes, your life is a gift from God. That's why self-nurturance is an expression of gratitude. When we take care of ourselves we show that we respect and value ourselves.

How do we nurture ourselves? Of all the blank spots we have, this one is often the most blank. If we've never seen, touched, tasted, or felt it, how can we know what nurturing is? Nurturing is an attitude toward ourselves—one of unconditional love and acceptance. I'm talking about loving ourselves so much and so hard that the good stuff gets right into the core of us, then spills over into our lives and our relationships. I'm talking about loving ourselves no matter what happens or where we go.

In the morning and throughout our day, we lovingly and gently ask ourselves what we can do for ourselves that would feel good. We ask ourselves what we need to do to take care of ourselves. We give ourselves encouragement and support. We tell ourselves we can do it, we can do it good enough, and things will work out. When we make a mistake, we tell ourselves that's okay. We wait a moment, until we get our balance back, then we ask ourselves if there's something we can learn from our mistake, or if there's some way we can improve our conduct in the future, or if there's an amend we need to make.

We tell ourselves we love and accept ourselves. We tell ourselves we're great and we're special. We tell ourselves we'll always be there for us. We make ourselves feel safe and loved. We do all those wonderful things for ourselves that we wish someone else had done for us.

If we don't believe we're lovable, why should anyone else? If I don't believe I'm lovable, I can't even believe my Higher Power loves me. If I don't believe I'm lovable, I don't let people, or God, love me. If we love ourselves, we're able to love others.

We stop criticizing and lambasting ourselves with harshness. Instead we make a conscious effort to nurture and praise ourselves, because it brings out the best in us.

"I've pushed myself all my life," says Arlene. "If I work hard, I tell myself to work harder. When I get tired, I push myself some more. I do and say all the critical things to myself that my mother did and said to herself and me."

Arlene worried that if she nurtured herself, the work wouldn't get done. She feared if she gave in to her needs, she'd get lazy. She decided to nurture herself anyway, and she was amazed.

"It was my day off. I was exhausted, but I was pushing myself to clean the house. Then I made a decision to nurture myself. I asked myself what would help me feel better, and I decided a nap would. I rested for two hours. When I woke up, I felt like doing the housework. I got it finished and even had time to go out that night. Nurturing myself didn't make me lazy or ineffective. It made me energized and more effective."

Nurturing is how we empower and energize ourselves. When we love, accept, and nurture ourselves, we can relax enough to do our best. A bonus is, when we love, accept, and nurture ourselves, we're able to do the same for others. We can help them love themselves, and they're more apt to react to us with love and acceptance. It starts a great chain reaction.

Loving and accepting ourselves unconditionally

doesn't mean we negate our need to change and grow. That's how we enable ourselves to love and grow.

There isn't a set of instructions for nurturing ourselves. But if we ask ourselves what would help us feel better or what we need, then listen, we'll hear the answer.

We can develop a way of life that embraces and blends the concepts of self-nurturing and self-discipline. We can love ourselves in all the ways we need and deserve to be loved. We can discipline ourselves in ways that will be in our own best interests.

DEVELOPING
SELF-DISCIPLINE

Self-discipline, like self-nurturance, is another clear expression of gratitude. When we're disciplined in positive ways, we're building on what we *know* we already have. And we're acting on the belief that if we're focused on our goals, the good stuff in life will continue to come our way.

Discipline is an individual process. Discipline means we don't always talk about feelings. Sometimes it's not appropriate, or sometimes we need to wait. Discipline means we go through the motions of positive behaviors on the gray days, the days we're uncertain whether anything is happening or if we're going anywhere on this journey. Discipline means we believe in our Higher Power in God's love for us, even when it might not look or feel as though God really does love us.

Discipline means we understand the cause-and-effect nature of things and choose behaviors that generate the consequences we desire. Discipline is self-control, but not the kind of control many of us have lived with. It's the kind we would teach a child we love very much, because we know that child needs to be able to do certain things in life to live a good life.

When will we become lovable? When will we feel safe?

When will we get all the protection, nurturing, and love we so richly deserve? We will get it when we begin giving it to ourselves.

Before I began working with affirmations, my first thought in the morning was, Oh, no. Not another day. It was downhill from there, until I dropped into bed at night, closed my eyes, and said, "Thank God that's over."

Now, when I open my eyes in the morning, I dwell on this thought for a moment: *This is the day the Lord has made. I will rejoice and be glad in it.*

A short time later, I say my morning prayers. While I'm brushing my teeth and putting on my makeup, I tell myself *out loud* that I love myself, I'll be there to take care of myself, God loves me and is taking care of me, I'm good at what I do, and all I need today shall be provided.

During morning break, I read from a meditation book. On my office desk there are several cards with uplifting sayings. At least every other day, I talk to a caring person to give and receive support, encouragement, and acceptance.

Throughout the day, I force-feed positive thoughts into my mind. When I feel ashamed, I tell myself it's okay to be who I am. When I have a feeling, I tell myself it's okay to feel. When I worry about money, I focus on this thought: *My God shall supply all my needs according to His riches in glory.*

I focus on a positive thought whenever a negative, fear-producing thought strikes. I also focus on positive thoughts during those odd moments when I would otherwise be concentrating on negative messages. If I feel panicky or desperate, I fill my mind with positive thoughts. I promise myself I'm safe.

I regularly write my goals. I write down what I believe I deserve. I spend an hour a week listening to meditation tapes. I spend a few minutes a week visualizing the good I want to happen. I see what it will look and feel like when it happens. I go in for a therapeutic massage regularly, and work on affirmations during that time. And I will gratitude for almost everything.

This is my regular routine. In times of stress, I

intensify my efforts. If this sounds like overkill, it isn't. Overkill was all the years I spent focusing on negative, destructive messages.

To discover what you need to work on, spend a day or two listening to your thoughts. Listen to what you say. Listen to the problems and negative qualities you empower in yourself and others. Look in the mirror and notice what you think and say. Sit down to pay bills and listen to your thoughts then. Go to your job and listen to what you think about your work, abilities, and career prospects.

Hold your special person in your arms and listen to your thoughts. Listen to how you react to your problems. Listen to what you say to and about your children. What are you giving power to? What are you creating space for? Are you feeding what you want to grow? Change what's needed and make it good. Declare all-out war on your destructive thought patterns. Embrace the belief that you can move from deprived to deserving.

Many of us have spent years nearly negating ourselves out of existence. Now we can learn to love ourselves into a life of our own.

Keep the Momentum Going

$\mathcal{N}$ow that you understand the gratitude principle and how affirmations can help you be more positive, it's important to keep the momentum going. In the upcoming pages I'll talk about how closely gratitude is tied to self-care and acceptance. I'll also talk about the importance of setting goals, respectful communication and making decisions in helping the good things in life come our way.

AN ATTITUDE OF SELF-CARE

I believe God has exciting, interesting things in store for each of us. I believe there is an enjoyable, worthwhile purpose for each of us. I believe we tap into this attitude by taking care of ourselves. We begin to cooperate. We open ourselves up to the goodness and richness available in us and to us.

Self-care is an attitude toward ourselves that says, I am responsible for myself and I'm grateful for my ability to take care of myself. I am responsible for leading my life. I am responsible for tending to my spiritual, emotional, physical, and financial well-being. I am responsible for identifying and meeting my needs. I am responsible for solving my problems and learning to live with those I cannot solve. I am responsible for my choices. I am responsible for what I give and receive.

I am also responsible for setting and achieving my goals. I am responsible for how much I enjoy life, for how much pleasure I find in daily activities. I am responsible for whom I choose to love and how I choose to express this love. I am responsible for what I do to others and for what I allow others to do to me. I am responsible for my wants and desires.

All of me, every aspect of my being, is important. I count for something. I matter. My feelings can be trusted. My thinking is appropriate. I value my wants and needs. I do not deserve and will not tolerate abuse or constant mistreatment. I have rights, and it is my responsibility to assert these rights. The decisions I make and the way I conduct myself will reflect my high self-esteem. My decisions will take into account my responsibilities to myself.

My decisions will also take into account my responsibilities to other people—my spouse, my children, my relatives, my friends. I will examine and decide exactly what these responsibilities are as I make my decisions. I will also consider the rights of those around me—their right to live their lives as they see fit. I do not have the right to impose on others' rights to take care of themselves, and they have no right to impose on my rights.

Self-care is an attitude of mutual respect. It means learning to live our lives responsibly. It means allowing others to live their lives as they choose, as long as they don't interfere with our decisions to live as we choose. Taking care of ourselves is not as selfish as some people assume it is, but neither is it as selfless as many others believe.

Your Needs Count

I believe that taking care of ourselves is an art, and this art involves one fundamental idea that is foreign to many: giving ourselves what we need.

This may be a shock to us and our families at first. Many of us don't ask for what we need. We don't know or haven't given much thought to what we want and need.

Many of us have falsely believed our needs aren't important and we shouldn't mention them. Some of us even began to believe our needs were bad or wrong, so we've learned to repress them and push them out of our awareness. We haven't learned to identify what we need, or listen to what we need because it didn't matter anyway—our needs weren't going to get met. Some of us haven't learned how to get our needs met appropriately.

Giving ourselves what we need is not difficult. I believe we can learn quickly. The formula is simple: In any given situation, detach and ask, "What do I need to do to take care of myself?"

Then we need to listen to ourselves and to our Higher Power. Respect what we hear. This insane business of punishing ourselves for what we think, feel, and want—this nonsense of not listening to who we are and what our selves are struggling to tell us—must stop.

How do you think God works with us? We can be gentle with ourselves and accept ourselves. We're not only or merely human, we were created and intended to be human. And we can be compassionate with ourselves. Then, perhaps, we may develop true compassion for others. Compassion for another person, by the way, is another expression of gratitude because this quality communicates that we really appreciate and respect his or her life. The people we have compassion for are often the people who teach us the greatest lessons.

Listen to what our precious self is telling us about what we need. Maybe we need to hurry and get to an appointment. Maybe we need to slow down and take the day off work. Maybe we need exercise or a nap. We might need to be alone. We may want to be around people. Maybe we need a job. Maybe we need to work less. Maybe we need a hug, or a kiss, or a back rub. Maybe we need to ask for one.

Sometimes giving ourselves what we need means giving ourselves something fun: a treat, a new hairdo, a new dress, a new pair of shoes, a new toy, an evening at the theater, or a trip to the Bahamas. Sometimes, giving ourselves what we need is work. We need to eliminate or develop a certain characteristic; we need to work on a relationship; or we need to tend to our responsibilities to other people or to our responsibilities to ourselves.

Giving ourselves what we need doesn't only mean giving presents to ourselves, it means doing what's necessary to live responsibly—not an excessively responsible or an irresponsible existence. With gratitude, we can learn to joyfully claim responsibility for ourselves and focus on what's good and right in our lives.

Our needs are different from moment to moment and from day to day. Are our thoughts negative and despairing? Maybe we need to read a meditation or inspiration book. Are we worried about a physical problem? Maybe we need to go to a doctor. Are the kids going wild? Maybe we need to figure out a family plan for discipline. Are people stomping on our rights? Maybe we need to set some boundaries. Are our stomachs churning with emotions? Maybe it's time to deal with our feelings. Maybe we need to detach, slow down. Maybe we need to initiate a relationship. It's up to us. What do we think we need to do?

Other People's Needs

In addition to giving ourselves what we need, we begin to ask other people for what we need and want from them because this is part of taking care of ourselves, part of being a responsible human being.

Giving ourselves what we need means we base all our decisions on reality, and we make them in our best interests. We take into account our responsibilities to other people, because that is what responsible people do. But we also know we count. We try to eliminate the "shoulds" from our decisions and learn to trust ourselves. If we listen to ourselves and our Higher Power, we will not be misled. Giving ourselves what we need and learning to live self-directed lives requires faith. We need enough faith to get on with our lives. We need to do at least a little something each day to begin moving forward. And getting in touch with gratitude is a good way to start.

As we learn how to care for and meet our own needs, we forgive ourselves when we make mistakes, and we congratulate ourselves when we do well. We develop gratitude for our efforts. We also get comfortable doing some things poorly and some things with mediocrity, for that is part of life too. We learn to laugh at ourselves and our humanity, but we don't laugh when we need to cry. We take ourselves seriously but not too seriously.

Ultimately, we may even discover this astounding truth: Few situations in life are ever improved by not taking care of ourselves, by not giving ourselves what we need. In fact, we may learn that most situations improve when we do take care of ourselves and tend to our needs.

I am learning to identify how to take care of myself. I know many people who have either learned or are learning to do this too. I believe that all of us can do it.

FACING THE "WHAT IF'S"

One of my common forms of self-torture involves a dilemma between two things to do. I make a decision to do one of them first. The minute I act on this decision, I say: "I should be doing the other thing." So I switch gears and begin doing the other thing. But then I start in on myself again: "I really shouldn't be doing this. I should be doing what I was doing before."

We find endless means of torturing ourselves: overeating, neglecting our needs, comparing ourselves to others, competing with people, obsessing, dwelling on painful memories, or imagining future painful scenes. We think, What if a tornado hits the house? What if I'm left without a job? This "what if" attitude is always good for a strong dose of fear. We scare ourselves, then wonder why we feel so frightened.

When these thoughts occur we need to stop them. Immediately! Then we can give ourselves a big emotional and mental hug. We tell ourselves we're okay. It's wonderful to be who we are. Our thoughts are okay. Our feelings are appropriate.

We're right where we're supposed to be today, this moment.

There is nothing wrong with us. There is nothing fundamentally wrong with us. If we've done wrongs, that's okay; we were doing the best we could. Despite our assorted character defects, we are okay. We are exactly as we are meant to be. And we're grateful for being who we are.

We can cherish ourselves and our lives. We can nurture ourselves and love ourselves. We can accept our wonderful selves, with all our faults, foibles, strong points, weak points, feelings, thoughts, and everything else. It's the best thing we've got going for us. It's who we are, and who we were meant to be. It's not a mistake. We are the greatest thing that will ever happen to us. Believe it. It makes life much easier.

We are good. We are good enough. We are appropriate to life. Much of our anxiety and fearfulness stems, I believe, from constantly telling ourselves that we're just not up to facing the world and all its situations. Well, I'm here to say we are indeed fit for reality. Relax. Wherever we need to go and whatever we need to do, we are appropriate for that situation. We will do fine. Relax. It's okay to be who we are. Who or what else can we be? Just do our best at whatever we are called upon to do. What more can we do?

Sometimes, we can't even do our best; that's okay, too. We may have feelings, thoughts, fears, and vulnerabilities as we go through life, but we all do. We need to stop telling ourselves we're different when we're actually doing and feeling what everyone else does.

We need to be good to ourselves. We need to be compassionate and kind to ourselves. How can we expect to take care of ourselves appropriately if we hate or dislike ourselves?

We need to value ourselves and make decisions and choices that enhance our self-esteem. And, yes, we need to be grateful for the choices that come our way. And we need to appreciate the many good decisions we've already made in our lives.

We can be gentle, loving, listening, attentive, and kind to ourselves, our feelings, thoughts, needs, wants, desires, and everything we're made of. We can accept ourselves—all of who we are. Start where you're at, and you will become more. Develop your gifts and talents and be grateful for these talents. Trust yourself. Assert yourself. You can be trusted. Respect yourself. Be true to yourself. Honor yourself, for that is where your magic lies. That is your key to the world.

We need to love ourselves and make a commitment to ourselves. We need to give ourselves some of the boundless loyalty that so many of us are willing to give others. Out of high self-esteem will come true acts of kindness and charity, not selfishness.

The love you give and receive will be enhanced by the love you give yourself.

THE ART
OF ACCEPTANCE

𝒜ccepting reality is an essential part of gratitude. Facing and coming to terms with *what is* is a beneficial act. Acceptance brings peace, and is frequently the turning point for change. But it is also much easier said than done.

People are faced daily with the prospect of either accepting or rejecting the reality of that particular day and present circumstances. We have many things to accept in the course of normal living from the moment we open our eyes in the morning until we close them at night. Our present circumstances include who we are, where we live, who we live with or without, where we work, our method of transportation, how much money we have, what our responsibilities are, what we're going to do for fun, and any problems that arise.

Some days, accepting these circumstances is a breeze. It comes naturally. Our hair behaves, our kids behave, the boss is reasonable, the money's right, the house is clean, the car works, and we like our spouse or lover. We know what to expect, and what we expect is acceptable. It's okay.

Other days might not go so well. The brakes go out on the car, the roof leaks, the kids sass, we break an arm, we lose our job, or our spouse or lover says he or she doesn't love us any more. Something has happened. We have a problem. Things are different. Things are changing. We're *losing* something. Our present circumstances are no longer as comfortable as they were. Circumstances have been altered, and we have a new situation to accept.

We may initially respond by denying or resisting the change, problem, or loss. We want things to be the way they were. We want the problem to be solved quickly. We want to be comfortable again. We want to know what to expect. We're not peaceful with reality. It feels awkward. We have temporarily lost our balance.

Some of us may have had our dreams and hopes crushed. Some of us may be facing the failure of something extremely important, such as marriage or another important relationship. I know there's a lot of pain at the prospect of losing love or losing the dreams we had. There's nothing we can say to make that less painful or to lessen our grief. It hurts deeply to have our dreams destroyed.

Yet, we must eventually come to terms with *what*

is. If things are ever to be any different, we must accept reality. If we are ever to replace our lost dreams with new dreams and feel peaceful again, we must accept reality.

Please understand, acceptance does not mean adaptation. It doesn't mean resignation to the sorry and miserable way things are. *It doesn't mean accepting or tolerating any sort of abuse.* Acceptance means that, for the present moment, we acknowledge and accept our circumstances, including ourselves and the people in our lives, as we are and they are. It is only from this state that we find the peace and the ability to evaluate these circumstances, to make appropriate changes, and to solve our problems.

If we're being abused, we will not make the decisions necessary to stop that abuse until we acknowledge the abuse. Then, we must stop pretending the abuse will somehow magically end. Stop pretending it doesn't exist. Stop making excuses for its existence.

In a state of acceptance we are able to respond responsibly to our environment. In this state we receive the power to change the things we can. We cannot change until we accept our powerlessness over the people and circumstances we have so desperately tried to control. Acceptance is the ultimate paradox: We cannot change who we are until we accept ourselves the way we are. When we surrender, when we're in a state of acceptance, we relinquish the need to resist ourselves and our environment. That's when we're free to cultivate contentment and gratitude.

It has also been my experience that my Higher Power seems reluctant to intervene in my circumstances until I accept what God has already given me. Acceptance is not forever. It is for the present moment. But to move beyond this moment, it must be sincere and at gut level.

The Process
of Acceptance

$\mathcal{H}$ow do we achieve this peaceful state? How do we stare at stark reality without blinking or covering our eyes? How do we accept all the losses, changes, and problems that life and people hurl at us? Not without a little kicking and screaming. In this respect, acceptance is like gratitude, we need to work at it. Even so, a natural process for acceptance is in place for us. Over the next few pages, I'll describe this process.

We accept things through a five-step process. Elisabeth Kübler-Ross first identified this process and its stages as the way terminally ill people accept their death—the ultimate loss. She called it the grief process. Since then, mental health professionals have observed that people go through these stages whenever they face any loss. The loss could be minor—a five dollar bill, not receiving an expected letter. Or the loss could be significant—the loss of a spouse through divorce or death, the loss of a job. Even positive changes, ones we're grateful for, can bring a sense of loss; for example, when we buy a new house and leave the old one.

Denial

The first stage of the process of acceptance is denial. This is a state of shock, numbness, panic, and general refusal to accept or acknowledge reality. We do everything and anything to put things back in place or pretend the situation isn't happening. There is much anxiety and fear in this stage. Reactions typical of denial include: refusing to believe reality ("No, this can't be!"); denying or minimizing the importance of the loss ("It's no big deal."); denying any feelings about the loss ("I don't care."); or mental avoidance (sleeping, obsessing, compulsive behaviors, and keeping busy). We may feel somewhat detached from ourselves, and our emotional responses may be flat, nonexistent, or inappropriate (laughing when we should be crying; crying when we should be happy).

The deep, instinctive part of us knows the truth, but we keep pushing that part away, telling it, "You're wrong. Shut up." According to counselor Scott Egleston, we then decide there's something fundamentally wrong with us for being suspicious, and we label ourselves and our innermost, intuitive being as untrustworthy.

Denial is the bugaboo of life. It's like being in a deep sleep. We aren't aware of our actions until we've done them. On some level, we really believe the lies *we* tell *ourselves.* But there is a reason for this.

Denial is the shock absorber for the soul. It is an instinctive and natural reaction to pain, loss, and change. It protects us. It wards off the blows of life until we can gather our other coping resources. In this respect, we don't need to beat ourselves up when we realize we've been in denial over a situation. We need to move on when the time is appropriate and appreciate the lessons we learn along the way.

Anger

When we have quit denying our loss, we move into the next stage: anger. Our anger may be reasonable or unreasonable. We may be justified in venting our wrath, or we may irrationally vent our fury on anything and anyone. We may blame ourselves, God, and everyone around us for what we have lost. Depending on the nature of the loss, we may be a little peeved, somewhat angry, downright furious, or caught in the grips of soul-shaking rage.

This is why setting someone straight, showing someone the light, or confronting a serious problem rarely turns out the way we expect. If we are denying a situation, we won't move directly into acceptance of reality—we move into anger. That is also why we need to be careful about major confrontations.

Bargaining

After we have calmed down, we attempt to strike a bargain with life, ourselves, another person, or God. If we do such and such or if someone else does this or that, then we won't have to suffer the loss. We are not attempting to postpone the inevitable; we are attempting to prevent it. Sometimes the deals we negotiate are reasonable and productive: "If my spouse and I get counseling, then we won't have to lose our relationship." Sometimes our bargains are absurd: "I used to think if I just kept the house cleaner or if I cleaned the refrigerator good enough this time, then my husband wouldn't drink any more," recalls the wife of an alcoholic.

Depression

When we see our bargain has not worked, when we finally become exhausted from our struggle to ward off reality, when we decide to acknowledge what life has socked to us we become very sad, sometimes terribly depressed. This is the essence of grief: mourning at its fullest. This is what we have been attempting at all costs to avoid. This is the time to cry, and it hurts. This stage of the process begins when we humbly surrender. The depression will disappear only when the process has been worked through.

Acceptance

After we have closed our eyes, kicked, screamed, negotiated, and finally felt the pain, we then arrive at the state of acceptance.

We are at peace with what is. We are free! We are free to stay, free to go on, free to make whatever decisions we need to make. We have accepted our loss, however minor or significant. It has become an acceptable part of our present circumstances. We are comfortable with it and our lives. We have adjusted and reorganized. Once more, we are comfortable with our present circumstances and ourselves.

Not only are we comfortable with our circumstances and the changes we have endured, but we believe we have in some way benefitted from our loss or change even if we cannot fully understand how or why. This is where gratitude comes in. We have faith that all is well, and we have grown from our experience. We deeply believe our present circumstances—all the details of them—are exactly as they ought to be for the moment. In spite of our fears, feelings, struggles, and confusion, we understand that everything is okay even if we lack insight. We accept what is. We settle down. We stop running, ducking, controlling, and hiding. And we know it is only from this point that we can go forward.

This is how people accept things. Some call it the grief process. Counselor Esther Olson also calls it the forgiveness process, the healing process, and the "way God works with us." It is not particularly comfortable. In fact, it is awkward and sometimes painful. We may feel as though we're falling apart. Whenever this process—whatever we choose to call it—begins, we usually feel shock and panic. As we go through the stages, we often feel confused, vulnerable, lonely, and isolated. A sense of loss of control is usually present, as is hope, which is sometimes unrealistic.

Over time we become familiar with this process. The whole thing may take place in thirty seconds for a minor loss. Or it may last years or a lifetime when the loss is significant. Because this is a model, we may not go through the stages exactly as I have outlined them. We may travel back and forth; from anger to denial, from denial to bargaining, from bargaining back to denial.

Regardless of the speed and route we travel through these stages, we must travel through them. It is not only a normal process, it is a necessary one, and each stage is necessary. We must ward off the blows of life with denial until we are better prepared to deal with them. We must feel anger and blame until we have gotten them out of our system. We must try to negotiate. And we must cry. We don't necessarily have to let the stages dictate our behaviors, but each of us, for our well-being and ultimate acceptance, needs to spend individually appropriate time in each stage.

We are sturdy beings. But in many ways, we are fragile. We can accept change and loss, but this comes at our own pace and in our own way. And only we and God can determine that timing.

We can give ourselves permission to go through this process when we face loss and change, even minor losses and changes. Be gentle with yourself. This is a draining, exhausting process. It can deplete your energy and throw you off balance. Watch how you pass through the stages and feel what you need to feel. Talk to people who are safe, people who will provide the comfort, support, and understanding you need.

Talk it out; talk it through. One thing that helps me is thanking God for the loss—for my present circumstances—regardless of how I feel or what I think about them. Another thing that helps many people is the Serenity Prayer.

> God grant me the serenity
> To accept the things I cannot change,
> The courage to change the things I can,
> And the wisdom to know the difference.

We don't have to act or behave inappropriately, but we need to go through this. Other people do, too. Understanding this process helps us be more supportive to other people, and it gives us the power to decide how we will behave and what to do to take care of ourselves when we go through it.

Set Your
Own Goals

*Believe that life is worth living
and your belief will create the fact.
Be not afraid to live.*

—William James

Once we begin to discover the good things in life, we naturally want to keep the momentum going. That's where goal setting comes in. There is magic in setting goals. Things happen. Things change. I accomplish important projects. I change. I meet new people. I find myself in interesting places. I make it through difficult times with a minimum of chaos. Problems get solved. My needs and wants get met. Dreams come true.

Goals are gratitude in action. They give us the opportunity to build on what we already have. While achieving goals can be a lengthy process, we can learn to be grateful for each stage in the process of setting and meeting goals.

I am ecstatic about goal setting, and I hope I can transmit my enthusiasm to you. There is nothing in the world like going where we want to go, getting what we want, solving a problem, or doing something we always wanted to do.

I'm not suggesting we can control all the events in our lives. We can't. We don't have final say on much of anything; God does. But I believe we can cooperate with goodness. I believe we can plan, make requests, and start a process in motion.

Goals give us direction and purpose. I don't get into my car, turn on the ignition, start driving, and hope I get someplace. I decide where I want to go, then I steer the car in that general direction. That is how I try to live my life, too. Sometimes things happen, and for a variety of reasons I may not end up where I wanted to go. If I change my mind or problems beyond my control interfere, I find myself doing something other than what I had planned to do.

Timing and exact circumstances may vary. That's okay. I usually end up someplace better or someplace that is better for me. That is where acceptance, gratitude, trust, faith, and letting go come in. But at least I'm not driving aimlessly through life. More of the things I want come to pass. I'm less worried about solving my problems, because I've turned my problems into opportunities that I'm grateful for.

And I'm starting to think about and consider what *I* want and need.

Goals are fun. They generate interest and enthusiam in life. They make life interesting and, sometimes, exciting.

There is magic in setting and writing down goals. It sets into motion a powerful psychological, spiritual, and emotional force. We become aware of and do the things we need to do to achieve and accomplish. Things come to us. Things begin to happen!

What are your goals? What do you want to happen in your life—this week, this month, this year, for the next five years? What problems do you want solved? What material things would you like to possess? What changes do you want to make in yourself? What would you love to do for a career? What do you want to accomplish?

I'm not going to present a textbook lecture on exactly how you should set goals. Setting goals has been made too boring for too long. Following are some ideas I believe are important. Find a way that works.

Turn everything into a goal. If you have a problem, make its solution your goal. You don't have to know the solution. Your goal is solving this problem. And be grateful for every step in achieving your goals.

Do you want something? A new waterbed, a red sweater, a new car, longer hair, longer nails? Turn it into a goal. Do you want to go someplace—Europe, South American, the circus? Do you want a loving, healthy relationship? Turn that into a goal. Is there something you've always wanted to do—go to school, work for a particular company, make $40,000 a year? Turn it into a goal. Do you need to decide upon a career? Turn making a decision into a goal. Do you want to grow closer to your Higher Power? Turn it into a goal.

Do you want to change something about yourself—learn to say no, make a particular decision, resolve some anger? Turn it into a goal. Do you want to improve your relationships with certain people—children, friends, spouse, a relative? Turn it into a goal. Do you want to form new relationships, lose weight, gain weight, quit worrying, stop controlling? Do you want to learn to have fun, learn to enjoy sex, achieve acceptance of some particular person or incident, forgive someone?

I believe we can successfully turn every aspect of our lives into a goal. If something bothers you, make it a goal. If you're aware that something needs to be changed, make it a goal. If you want it, make it a goal.

Omit the shoulds. We have enough shoulds controlling our lives; we don't need them in our goals. Make it a goal to get rid of 75 percent of your shoulds.

Don't limit yourself. Go for all of it—everything you want and need, all the problems you want solved, all your desires, and even some of your whims. Don't worry. If you're not supposed to have it, you won't. If you are supposed to have it, I believe you'll stand an improved chance of getting it by turning it into a goal.

Write your goals on paper. There is extraordinary power in jotting down goals, rather than storing them loosely in your mind. You worry less, and it gives focus and organization to your goals. Recording your goals also helps direct your energy and put you in contact with your Higher Power. You don't have to write your goals neatly or perfectly, or use particular words or systems. Commit them to paper—all of them.

Commit your written goals to God. Tell God these are the things you're interested in, ask for His help, then surrender humbly. This process is called, "Thy will be done—not mine."

Let go. Keep your goals close by, somewhere that you can look at them as you need to. But don't worry and obsess about how, when, if, and what if. Some people suggest that we monitor our goals daily. I don't, except when I'm setting daily goals. But you can do it any way you choose. Once my goals are on paper, I try to not control or force.

Do what you can, one day at a time. Within the framework of each twenty-four-hour day, do what seems fitting and appropriate. Do God's will for that day. Do what you are inspired to do. Do what comes your way that needs to be done. Do it in peace and faith. Do it with gratitude. Marvelous things can and do come to pass this way. Try it. You have to do your part. But I believe we can and will do our part best by doing it *one day at a time.* If it's time to do something, we'll know. If it's time for something to happen, it will. Trust yourself and trust God.

Set goals regularly and as needed. I like to do my annual goals at the beginning of each new year. It tells me that I am interested in living my life that particular year. I don't believe in New Year's resolutions; I believe in goals. I also write down goals as they occur to me throughout the year. If I am facing a problem, spot a need, feel a new want, I turn it into a goal and add it to my list. I also use goals to get me through crisis times, when I'm feeling shaky. Then I write down all the things I want and need to accomplish on a daily, weekly, or monthly basis.

Check off the goals you reach. Yes, you will start reaching your goals. Your wants and needs will get met. You will achieve certain things that are important to you. When this happens, cross off the goal, congratulate yourself, and thank God. You will gain confidence in yourself, in goal setting, in God, and in the rhythm of life this way. You will see for yourself that good things do happen.

Sometimes, we may experience a letdown when we reach a goal, especially if it's been an important goal that required much energy, or if we've done "magical thinking" about reaching it. Magical thinking includes thoughts such as, "I will live happily ever after once this problem is solved," or "I will live happily ever after once I get a waterbed." To avoid a let down, it's important to have a long list of goals and to avoid magical thinking. I've never yet reached a goal or solved a problem that has enabled me to live happily ever after. Life goes on, and I try to live happily and peacefully day to day.

We may never be without a list of problems that we need to turn into goals. We will probably never be without wants and needs. But this process of goal setting, besides making life more enjoyable, helps develop a certain faith and gratitude in the ebb and flow and general goodness of life. Problems arise. Problems get solved. Wants and needs come into awareness. Wants and needs get met. Dreams are born. Dreams are reached. Things happen. Good things happen. Then, more problems arise. But it's all okay.

Be patient. Trust in God's timing. Don't take an item off the list just because you didn't achieve or receive something when you thought you should have—

those wretched "shoulds" infiltrate every area of life. Sometimes my goals carry over for years. When I do my annual goal setting, I sometimes look at my sheet and think, Oh, this problem will never get solved. It's been on my list for years. Or, this dream will never come true. It's the fourth year in a row I've written it down. Or, I'll never be able to change this character defect of mine. Not true. It just hasn't happened yet.

Things happen when the time is right—when we're ready, when God is ready, when the world is ready. Give up. Let go. But keep it on the list.

We need to set goals for ourselves. Start today— when you put down this book. If you don't have any goals, make your first goal "getting some goals." You probably won't start living happily ever after, but you may start living happily, purposefully, and with gratitude.

COMMUNICATION

When we move from a place of feeling deprived to a place of feeling deserving, we realize the importance of respectful communication.

Communication is not mystical. The words we speak reflect who we are: what we think, judge, feel, value, honor, love, hate, fear, desire, hope for, believe in, and commit to.

Talking clearly and openly is not difficult. In fact, it's easy and fun. Start by knowing that who you are is okay. Your feelings and thoughts are okay. Your opinions count. It's okay to talk about your problems. And it's okay to say no.

You *can* say no—whenever you want to. It's easy. Say it right now. Ten times. See how easy that was? By the way, other people can say no, too. It makes it easier if we've got equal rights. Whenever your answer is no, start your response with the word *No*, instead of saying, "I don't think so," or "Maybe," or some other wavering phrase.

Say what you mean, and mean what you say. If you don't know what you mean, be quiet and think about it. If your answer is "I don't know," say "I don't know." Learn to be concise. Stop taking people all around the block. Get to the point, and when you make it, stop.

Talk about problems. We're not being disloyal to anyone by revealing who we are and what kinds of problems we're working on. All we're doing is pretending by not being who we are. Share secrets with trusted friends who won't use these against you or make you feel ashamed. We can make appropriate decisions about who to talk to, how much to tell them, and when to talk to them.

Express your feelings: openly, honestly, appropriately, and responsibly. Let others do the same. Learn the words: "I feel." Let others say those words and learn to listen when they do.

We can say what we think. Learn to say: "This is what I think." Our opinions can be different than other people's opinions. That doesn't mean we're wrong. We don't have to change our opinions, and neither does the other person, unless either of us wants to.

We can even be wrong. It's okay to be wrong. And to say so.

We can say what we expect, without demanding

that other people change to suit our needs. Other people can say what they expect, and we don't have to change to suit them, either—if we don't want to.

We can express our wants and needs. Learn the words: "This is what I need from you. This is what I want from you."

We can tell the truth. Lying about what we think, how we feel, and what we want isn't being polite—it's lying.

We don't have to be controlled by what other people say. We don't have to try to control them with our words and special effects. We don't have to be manipulated, coerced, made to feel guilty, or forced into anything. We can open our mouths and take care of ourselves! Learn to say: "I love you, but I love me, too. This is what I need to do to take care of *me.*"

We can be assertive and stand up for ourselves without being abrasive or aggressive. Learn to say: "This is as far as I go. This is my limit. I will not tolerate this." And mean those words.

We can show compassion and concern without rescuing. Learn to say, "Sounds like you're having a problem. What do you need from me?" Learn to say,

"I'm sorry you're having that problem." Then, let it go. We don't have to fix it.

We can discuss our feelings and problems without expecting people to rescue us, too. We can settle for being listened to. That's probably all we ever wanted anyway.

Take yourself seriously. Balance that with an appropriate sense of humor and you won't have to worry about what anyone else is or isn't doing.

Learn to listen to what people are saying and not saying. Learn to listen to yourself, the tone of your voice, the words you choose, the way you express yourself, and the thoughts going through your mind. Learn to appreciate your words.

Talking is a tool and a delight. We talk to express ourselves. We talk to be listened to. Talking enables us to understand ourselves and helps us understand other people. Talking helps us get messages to people. Sometimes we talk to achieve closeness and intimacy. Maybe we don't always have something Earth shattering to say, but we want connect with people. We want to bridge the gap. We want to share and be close. Sometimes we talk to have fun— to play, enjoy, banter, and entertain.

There are times when we talk to take care of ourselves—to make it clear that we will not be bullied or abused, that we love ourselves, and that we have made decisions in our best interests. And then there are the times we just talk.

We need to take responsibility for communication. Let your words reflect high self-esteem and esteem for others. Be honest. Be direct. Be open. Be gentle and loving when that's appropriate. Be firm when the situation calls for firmness. Above all else, be who you are and say what you need to say.

In love and dignity, speak the truth—as you think, feel, and know it—and it shall set you free.

MAKING DECISIONS

"*W*hat do *you* think I should do?" a client asked me.

"What do *you* think?" I asked.

"You're asking *me*?" she asked. "It takes me fifteen minutes at the grocery store to decide if I want to buy the 59-cent or the 63-cent bottle of bleach. I can't make the tiniest decisions. How do you expect me to make a big important one like this?"

Many of us don't trust our minds. We truly understand the horror of indecision. The smallest choices, such as what to order at the restaurant or which bottle of bleach to purchase, paralyze us. And the big significant decisions we face—such as how to solve our problems, what to do with our lives, and who to live with—can overwhelm us. Many of us simply give up and refuse to think about these things. Some of us allow other people or circumstances to make these choices for us.

For a variety of reasons, we may sometimes lose faith in our ability to think and reason things out. Believing lies, lying to ourselves (denial), chaos, stress, low self-esteem, and a stomach full of repressed emotions may cloud our ability to think. We become confused. That doesn't mean we *can't* think.

Overreacting may impair our mental functioning. Decisiveness is hindered by worrying about what other people think, telling ourselves we have to be perfect, telling ourselves to hurry. We falsely believe we must not make the "wrong" choice, that we'll never have another chance, that the whole world rides on this particular decision. We don't have to do these things to ourselves.

Hating ourselves, telling ourselves we won't make good decisions, and then throwing in a batch of "shoulds" every time we try to make decisions, doesn't help our thinking process either.

Not listening to our needs and wants, and telling ourselves that what we desire is wrong, cheats us out of the information we need to make good choices. Second-guessing and "what ifs" don't help either. We're learning to love, trust, and listen to ourselves.

Maybe we've been using our minds inappropriately, to worry and obsess, and our minds are tired, abused, and filled with anxious thoughts. We're learning how to stop these patterns also.

Perhaps we've lost faith in our ability to think and

make good decisions because people have told us we can't. Our parents may have done this directly or indirectly when we were children. They may have told us we were stupid. Or they may have made all our decisions for us. Maybe they criticized all our choices. Or they could have confused us by denying or by refusing to acknowledge our ability to think when we pointed out problems in the home.

People may have put down the intelligence of women, but that's nonsense. Women can think. Men can think. Children can think.

We can think. Our minds work well. We can figure things out. We can make decisions. We can figure out what we want and need to do and when it is time to do that. And we can make choices that enhance our self-esteem. A big part of gratitude is appreciating our minds.

We're even entitled to opinions! And yes, we do have some of those. We can think appropriately and rationally. We have the power to evaluate ourselves and our thoughts, so we can correct our thinking when it becomes disastrous or irrational.

We can evaluate our behavior. We can make decisions about what we need and want. We can figure out what our problems are and what we need to do to solve them. We can make little decisions and big decisions. We may feel frustrated when we face decisions or solve problems, but that's normal. Sometimes we need to become frustrated in order to make a breakthrough in our thinking. It's all part of the process.

Remember, decisions don't have to be made perfectly. We don't have to be perfect. We don't even have to be nearly perfect. We can just be who we are. We can make mistakes in our choices. We're not so fragile that we can't handle making a mistake. It's no big deal! It's part of living. We can learn from our mistakes, or we can simply make another decision.

We can even change our minds. Then change them again. Then again. We may go back and forth a lot. This is how we get to where we're going. It's okay—it's normal and often necessary.

The following suggestions may help you gain confidence in your mental abilities.

Treat your mind to some peace. Detach. Get calm. If you're facing a decision, big or small, get peaceful first, then decide. If you absolutely can't make a decision on a particular day, then it's obviously not time to make that decision. When it is time, you'll be able to do it. And do it well.

Ask God to Help you think. Every morning, I ask Him to give me the right thought, word, or action. I ask Him to send His inspiration and guidance. I believe He does help. I know He does. But He expects me to do my part and think. Some days go better than others.

Quit abusing your mind. Worry and obsession constitute mental abuse. Stop doing those things.

Feed your mind. Give your mind information. Get the information you need about problems and decisions, whether that problem is related to health, relationships, or how to buy a computer. Give your mind a reasonable amount of data, then sort through things. You will come up with good answers and solutions.

Feed your mind healthy thoughts. Indulge in activities that uplift your thoughts and give you a positive charge. Read a meditation book every morning. Find something that leaves you saying "I can," instead of "I can't."

Stretch your mind. Many of us become so concerned about our problems and other people's problems that we stop reading newspapers, watching documentaries, reading books, and learning new things. Get interested in the world around you. Learn something new. Take a class.

Quit saying bad things about your mind. As I've discussed already, we can stop telling ourselves things like, "I'm stupid," "I can't make good decisions," "I'm really not very smart," "I've never been good at figuring things out," or "I'm not very good at decisions." It's just as easy to say good things about yourself as it is to say negative things. And, you'll probably start believing the positive things and find out they're true. Isn't that exciting?

Use your mind. Make decisions. Formulate opinions. Express them. Create! Think things through, but don't worry and obsess. We don't have to let anyone make our decisions for us, unless we're wards of the state. And even if we are, we can still think and make some of our choices.

Letting people make our decisions for us means we're getting rescued, which means we're feeling like victims. We're not victims. Furthermore, it is not our business to make decisions for other adults. We can take possession of our power to think, and really appreciate this power. And we can let others be responsible for their thinking. We will gain more confidence in ourselves, as we start feeling better and begin to make decisions, small and large. The people around us will grow, as they are allowed to make choices and mistakes.

We can become comfortable with our minds. Become acquainted with them. They're part of us, and they work. Trust them and your ability to think.

EXPECT GOOD THINGS

I hope my ideas help you affirm and expect good things—for yourself and your loved ones.

When you wonder what is coming, tell yourself the best is coming, the very best life and love have to offer, the best God and His universe have to send. Then open your hands to receive it. Claim it, and it is yours.

See the best in your mind. Envision what it will look like, what it will feel like. Focus, until you can see it clearly. Let your whole being, body and soul, enter into and hold onto the image for a moment.

Then, let it go. Come back into today, the present moment. Do not obsess. Do not become fearful. Become excited. Live today fully, expressing gratitude for all you have been, all you are right now, and all you are becoming.

Say "thank you" for all things—and expect good things.

ABOUT THE AUTHOR

Melody Beattie is the author of *Codependent No More*, *Beyond Codependency*, *The Language of Letting Go*, and *Codependents' Guide to the Twelve Steps*. She lives in Minneapolis, Minnesota.